MW00568925

About
Skill Builders
Spelling

by Rosemarie Howard

Welcome to RBP Books' Skill Builders series. Like our Summer Bridge Activities collection, the Skill Builders series is designed to make learning both fun and rewarding.

This workbook is based on core curriculum and designed to reinforce classroom spelling skills and strategies for third graders. This workbook holds students' interest with the right mix of challenge, imagination, and instruction. The diverse assignments teach spelling while giving the students something fun to think about—from crooks to campouts. As students complete the workbook, they will be well prepared to challenge themselves with more difficult words and vocabulary.

A critical thinking section includes exercises to help develop higher-order thinking skills.

Learning is more effective when approached with an element of fun and enthusiasm—just as most children approach life. That's why the Skill Builders combine entertaining and academically sound exercises with eye-catching graphics and fun themes—to make reviewing basic skills at school or home fun and effective, for both you and your budding scholars.

Table of Contents

Days of the Week

Matt and Denise learned this poem about the days of the week. Unscramble the day of the week under each line. Write the word in the blank; then read the poem. Be sure to begin each sentence and each day of the week with a capital letter.

1. __Monday's__ child is fair of face.
   dya'snom

2. _____ child is full of grace.
   uesdayt's

3. _____ child is full of woe.
   desnedwyas'

4. _____ child has far to go.
   'sythurdsa

5. _____ child is loving and giving.
   dirfays'

6. _____ child works hard for his living.
   atdaursy's

7. And the lucky child born on the _____ day
   abbaths
   is handsome and happy and sings on his way.

1

More Days of the Week

Circle the correct spelling of each day of the week to complete each sentence. Write the correctly spelled word in the blank.

1. Many people go to church on _____.
   (Sunday/Sundai)

2. _____ (Munday/Monday) used to be the day for washing clothes.

3. Before wash-and-wear clothes were invented, _____ (Tuesday/Twosday) was the day women would iron clothes.

4. _____ (Wensday/Wednesday) was named after the Norse god Odin, who was also called Woden.

5. Thanksgiving Day is always on _____.
   (Thursday/Thirsday)

6. Some people think _____ (Fryday/Friday) the thirteenth is an unlucky day.

7. _____ (Saterday/Saturday) is named after the Roman god Saturn, who was god of the harvest.

2

Days of the Week— Abbreviations

Matt is sometimes in a hurry and uses abbreviations, or a shorter way, to write the days of the week. Write the correct abbreviation for each day of the week in the blank after the day's name.

1. Sunday   **Sun.**_____

2. Monday   _____

3. Tuesday   _____

4. Wednesday _____

5. Thursday   _____

6. Friday   _____

7. Saturday   _____

Write a riddle or poem about your favorite day of the week.

Example:

The week doesn't end or begin with me.
My name's in the middle
And I start with "we."
Which day of the week am I?
(Answer: Wednesday)

_____
_____
_____
_____
_____
_____

© RBP Books   Spelling Grade 3—RBP075X

Days of the Week Word Search

Find the names of each day of the week in the word search. Use the Word Bank to help you remember the names. Write each word on the lines below.

Monday   Tuesday   Wednesday   Thursday
Friday   Saturday   Sunday

```
c t h u r s d a y u
r y a d s e u t y u
a e y e t k o a d q
y e a a g n d j f n
a n s b d s n q c h
d v u p e r v p y b
n q n n k l u s w k
o z d q b w k t c l
m e a u q v l x a p
w x y f r i d a y s
```

_____ _____ _____

_____ _____ _____

_____ _____ _____

_____ _____ _____

_____

The 12 Months of the Year

Write the names of each month in the column that shows the number of days that month has.

Matt and Denise use this poem to remember how many days are in each month.

Thirty days hath September,
April, June, and November;
All the rest have thirty-one,
Excepting February alone,
And that has twenty-eight days clear
And twenty-nine in each leap year.

January	February	March	April
May	June	July	August
September	October	November	December

30 Days	31 Days	28/29 Days

_____   _____   _____

_____   _____   _____

_____   _____   _____

_____   _____

              _____

              _____

Use the Word Bank on page 5 to help solve the crossword puzzle about the months of the year.

ACROSS

3. Mexican people celebrate the fifth day of this month.

6. Labor Day is celebrated on the first Monday of this month.

8. The first month of the year is called _____.

9. The abbreviation for this month is Aug.

10. The USA celebrates its birthday in this month.

11. Many people celebrate Christmas in this month.

DOWN

1. Thanksgiving Day is the last Thursday of this month.

2. This month is the shortest month of the year.

4. An old saying says, "_____ showers bring May flowers."

5. St. Patrick's Day is on the 17th day of this month.

7. Halloween is celebrated in this month.

10. The first day of summer is in this month.

Months of the Year— Abbreviations

Match each month with its correct abbreviation.

January	May
February	Dec.
March	Jan.
April	Oct.
May	Sept.
June	Feb.
July	Nov.
August	Apr.
September	June
October	July
November	Aug.
December	Mar.

 Spelling Grade 3—RBP075X

The Seasons: Spring, Summer, Fall, Winter

Spring Riddle

Denise loves spring because of the daffodils. This is one of her favorite spring riddles.
Circle the rhyming words at the end of each sentence. Then make a list of other words that rhyme and end in **-own** or the **long o** sound on the blanks under the riddle.

Daffy-down-dilly is now come to town
With a petticoat green and a bright yellow gown.

What is the riddle about?

_____

<u>Words that end in -*own*</u>   <u>Words that end in the long *o* sound</u>

1. _____ 1. _____
2. _____ 2. _____
3. _____ 3. _____
4. _____ 4. _____
5. _____ 5. _____

Use the words to write your own springtime riddle on the lines below. Check your spelling!

_____
_____
_____

Spring Poem

Matt and Denise both like this springtime poem about a robin that outsmarts a cat.

1. Read the poem aloud.
2. Circle the correctly spelled word choices in each line.
3. Underline all the rhyming words.

Little Robin Redbreast (sat/sate) upon a tree,

Up (whent/went) Kitty Cat and (down/doune) went he;

Down (came/caime) Kitty, and away Robin (ranne/ran);

Says (little/leetle) Robin Redbreast, "(Kach/Catch) me if you

can."

Little Robin Redbreast (jumped/jumt) upon a (wahl/wall),

Kitty Cat jumped after (hym/him) and almost (got/gat) a fall;

Little Robin chirped and sang, and (wot/what) did Kitty say?

Kitty Cat (said/sed), "Mew," and Robin jumped (uhwey/away).

9

Spelling Grade 3—RBP075X

Spider Poem

Spiders are some of Matt's favorite bugs. He likes to watch them spin their webs. This is a poem he likes about a spider.

1. Read the poem aloud.
2. Circle all the words with long vowel sounds.
3. Write the words you circled on the lines below the poem. You may write some of the words more than once.

An eency, weency spider climbed up the water spout.

Down came the rain and washed the spider out.

Out came the sun and dried up all the rain,

So the eency weency spider went up the spout again.

1. _____   8. _____

2. _____   9. _____

3. _____   10. _____

4. _____   11. _____

5. _____   12. _____

6. _____   13. _____

7. _____

Spider Word Search

Find the words you wrote in the blanks after the
poem "Eency, Weency Spider" in the word search
below. Each word is used only one time.

```
r c i q e u d l m e v y b
v l t z b e d r a i n p l
m i k z i a y r e d i p s
w m m r q c i m l n q a z
b b d y n k w f q d n q i
q e w e t r j n h u w a s
v d e r e w w a e j h b b
r i w v m h c e b l f c h
w e k e a v c c e r i p i
f u c a c n b n m n p g n
q s j k e k x g s c c y u
u h q v f k h t h a f y b
```

Spelling Grade 3—RBP075X

Long Vowels

Denise loves springtime. Circle the correctly spelled word in each sentence below. Write the word in the blank. All of the words have the same long vowel sounds you circled in the poem about the spider.

1. On the first day of spring, the sky was not (bright/brite) _____. It was cloudy.

2. Denise decided to go for a walk in the (rein/rain) _____.

3. She wanted to (try/trie) _____ her new raincoat and umbrella.

4. It was not raining hard, and the air smelled fresh and (clean/clene) _____.

5. The (leaves/leeves) _____ on the tree by her house were beginning to unfold.

6. Denise splashed in the puddles with (delite/delight) _____.

7. She saw a mother bird with a worm in her (beak/beek) _____.

8. A (ray/rai) _____ of sunshine broke through the clouds.

9. Denise looked up to see a beautiful (ranebough/rainbow) _____ shining over her head.

10. That made Denise (smile/smiel) _____ as she ran home to have a cup of hot chocolate.

The Queen of Hearts

Matt likes this summer poem about a queen's servant who really liked tarts. Use the dictionary to learn what kind of food a "tart" is. Write the definition of "tart" on the line below. Then circle the correctly spelled word below.

The Queen of (Harts/Hearts),

She (made/maid) some (tarhts/tarts),

All on a summer's (day/daye).

The (Nave/Knave) of Hearts,

He (stole/stoal) those (tarhts/tarts)

And took them clean (aweigh/away).

The (King/Keeng) of Hearts

Called for the (tarhts/tarts)

And (beet/beat) the Knave full (soar/sore).

The Knave of Hearts

(Brought/Braught) back the (tarhts/tarts)

And vowed he'd (steel/steal) no (moor/more).

Homophone Crossword

Solve the crossword puzzle using the words in the Word Bank. They are homophones, words that sound alike but are spelled differently and have different meanings.

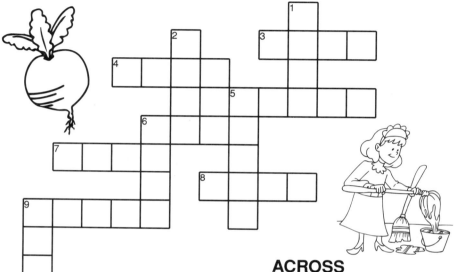

Word Bank

beet
soar
hart
made
steel
moor
more
maid
heart
steal
sore
beat

ACROSS

3. a wet land where heather grows
4. a word that means "to fly"
5. a very strong metal
6. a red vegetable
7. May I have some _____?
8. a person who cleans for a living
9. the organ that pumps your blood

DOWN

1. a wound or hurt
2. a word that means "created"
5. to take something that isn't yours
6. to hit a drum
9. another word for *deer*

At the Beach

Matt and Denise love to spend time at the beach during the summer. This story tels what happened to Matt the first time he went to the beach this summer. Circle the correct word choice in each sentence. Write the correct word in the blank.

1. Matt spent the day at the (beech/beach)
   _____.

2. The sun didn't (seam/seem) _____ very bright.

3. He forgot to (ware/wear) _____ sunscreen.

4. He went swimming in the (see/sea) _____.

5. (By/Buy) _____ the time he went home, he felt very hot.

6. His face was as red as a (beat/beet) _____.

7. His back was also red and (soar/sore) _____.

8. Even his (feet/feat) _____ were sunburned.

9. "You (know/no) _____ you should (wear/ware) _____ sunscreen, Matt," his mother said when she saw him.

10. "I forgot," replied Matt, "but I will (not/knot) _____ forget next time!"

Summertime Fun

Matt and Denise like to cook. A Purple Cow is one of their favorite summertime drinks. Match the cooking words below with their abbreviations. Then write the words on the line after their abbreviations. For a treat, try making a Purple Cow.

1. ounce   Tbsp.

2. teaspoon   c.

3. tablespoon   oz.

4. cup   l

5. pound   tsp.

6. liter   lb.

tsp.   _____

oz.   _____

l   _____

Tbsp. _____

Purple Cow

$\frac{1}{2}$ can (3 oz.) grape juice concentrate

1 c. milk

2 c. vanilla ice cream

Pour juice concentrate and milk into blender. Scoop in ice cream. Cover and blend on high speed for 30 seconds. Serve immediately. Makes 3 servings, or 1 or 2 big shakes.

What's Cooking?

Use the Word Bank to locate the Purple Cow cooking words in the word search below.

cup	serving	teaspoon	scoop
tablespoon	shake	ounce	ice
cream	mix	juice	blend
milk	stir	pour	

```
a h a l w x n o o p s a e t k z d
r w s c o o p q x o f o e c i u j
y z l z c y q i y c o c u p c g x
b o c r s c m t a b l e s p o o n
q m e u h g n i v r e s x i n e t
k a n o a d n e l b e z t r i t s
m q y p k f n g d r b e c n u o n
n l g q e c i k l i m k y g m s r
```

© RBP Books

Wishing on Summer Stars

Sometimes when Denise sees the first star in the evening sky, she says this poem and makes a wish. Circle all the words in the poem that end in the **long i** sound made by **-ight**.

Star light, star bright,
First star I see tonight,
I wish I may, I wish I might
Have the wish I wish tonight.

Make a list of other words you know that end in the long *i* sound. Use a dictionary to check your spelling if you need to.

_____   _____

_____   _____

_____   _____

Write your own poem about stars or nighttime using some of the words you wrote on the lines above. Follow the pattern (four lines, each line rhymes with the same sound) of the "Star Light" poem. Be sure to check your spelling.

_____

_____

_____

_____

_____

_____

_____

A Summer Campout

Denise and her parents like to go camping during the summer. Fill in the blank in each sentence to make words ending in the **long i** sound made by **-ight**. Use the letters in the Word Bank.

to	r	l	sl	l	s	t	n	br	fl

1. _____night the family will camp under the stars.

2. Mom hopes the weather is _____ight for camping.

3. The weatherman says there is a _____ight chance of showers.

4. If it does rain, Dad hopes the tent is water_____ight.

5. Denise's dad helps her find star pictures in the _____ight sky.

6. He says Venus looks like a very _____ight star.

7. Some people would like to take a _____ight to the moon.

8. Denise's parents like to walk in the moon_____ight.

9. "The moon shining on the water is a beautiful _____ight," says Mom.

10. "It's time to turn out the _____ight and go to sleep," says Dad.

© RBP Books   Spelling Grade 3—RBP075X

Fall Poem

Read the poem aloud. Circle the words with the **long e** sound. Underline the words with the **short e** sound.

Peter, Peter, pumpkin eater,
Had a wife and couldn't keep her.
He put her in a pumpkin shell,
And there he kept her very well.

Peter, Peter, pumpkin eater,
Had another and didn't love her;
Peter learned to read and spell,
And then he loved her very well.

Work the word puzzle to spell some of the words that you read in the poem. Write the new word in the blank.

1. bell – b + w =   **well**
2. spend – nd + ll = _____
3. sleep – sl + k = _____
4. heater – h = _____
5. knife – kn + w = _____
6. slept – sl + k = _____
7. mother – m + an = _____
8. spell – sp + sh = _____
9. shoved – sh + l = _____
10. teeter – te + P = _____
11. bead – b + r = _____
12. bumpkin – b + p = _____
13. sad – s + h = _____
14. every – e = _____

The Pumpkin Patch

To learn about Matt and Denise's adventure in a pumpkin patch, unscramble the words in parentheses. Write the correctly spelled word in the blank. Use the Word Bank to help you spell the words correctly.

home	choose	pumpkin	between
under	crop	take	fence
huge	small	vines	dead

1. George took Matt and Denise to a (upkinpm) _____ patch.

2. Each of them got to (esooch) _____ a pumpkin.

3. The (proc) _____ of pumpkins was ripe.

4. The pumpkin (sinev) _____ were (edad) _____ and brown.

5. Denise wanted to carve a (amsll) _____ jack-o-lantern.

6. Matt chose a (ehug) _____ pumpkin.

7. Denise found just the right pumpkin next to the (nefce) _____.

8. Matt found the one he wanted (weentbe) _____ two bales of hay.

9. George found his pumpkin (nuedr) _____ a tree.

10. As it began to get dark, they decided it was time to (keta) _____ their pumpkins (mhoe) _____.

Tongue Twister

Denise and Matt like to say tongue twisters as quickly as they can. Try saying this tongue twister.

Peter Piper picked a peck of pickled peppers;

A peck of pickled peppers Peter Piper picked;

If Peter Piper picked a peck of pickled peppers,

Where's the peck of pickled peppers Peter Piper picked?

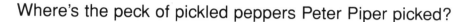

Choose a consonant and write six words that begin with that consonant. Write your own tongue twister using those words.

Example:

Sally	song	sat
simple	sew	silly

Simple Sally sang a silly song as she sat and sewed.

Your words:

_____ _____ _____

_____ _____ _____

Your tongue twister:

_____

_____

_____

www.summerbridgeactivities.com ©RBP Books

Sleepy Hollow

Denise and Matt like to carve pumpkins and read scary stories on Halloween. Use the Word Bank to fill in the blanks in the story.

bell	pumpkin	well	spell
very	read	keep	wife
loved	kept	shell	

1. Matt carved his jack-o-lantern from a huge _____.

2. Denise's pumpkin was _____ small.

3. After they carved the jack-o-lanterns, George _____ "The Legend of Sleepy Hollow."

4. Matt and Denise _____ the story about a man named Ichabod, who believed in ghosts.

5. He taught school and began each day by ringing a _____.

6. He _____ a book about magic in his backpack.

7. Ichabod believed a magic _____ could harm him.

8. Ichabod thought he could sing very _____.

9. Ichabod wanted a beautiful girl named Katrina to become his _____.

10. Katrina decided to _____ her old boyfriend, Brom, and not marry Ichabod.

11. At the end of the story, a broken pumpkin _____ was found on the road by the church cemetery.

© RBP Books

Wee Willie Winkie

Matt, Denise, and their friends always get excited about the first day of school. Going to school also means going to bed early. Read the poem below aloud. Then circle the compound words in the poem.

Wee Willie Winkie runs through the town,

Upstairs and downstairs in his nightgown,

Rapping at the window, crying through the lock,

"Are the children in their beds, for now it's eight o'clock?"

Draw a line between the two words that make each compound word below. Then write each word on the lines beside the compound word.

1. mid|night   __mid__   __night__
2. daylight   _____ _____
3. moonlight   _____ _____
4. nightgown   _____ _____
5. cartwheel   _____ _____
6. playground   _____ _____
7. breakfast   _____ _____
8. daybreak   _____ _____
9. afternoon   _____ _____
10. stairway   _____ _____
11. everybody   _____ _____
12. anything   _____ _____
13. classroom   _____ _____
14. sidewalk   _____ _____
15. chalkboard   _____ _____

Unscramble the words in parentheses. Then write the words in the blanks.

1. (vreybdEyo) _____ was excited to go to school on the first day.

2. Matt did a (eelwhtcra) _____ in the backyard.

3. Denise couldn't fall asleep until (igthmidn) _____.

4. They were both up at (kreabdya) _____ to get ready for school.

5. Matt had pancakes for (astfreakb) _____.

6. Denise found her new (oomlassrc) _____ easily.

7. The teacher wrote her name on the (kahlcroadb) _____.

8. Denise and Matt had fun on the (ylaprognud) _____ at recess.

9. That (fteraoonn) _____ after school, Denise was tired.

10. Denise put on her (owngihgtn) _____ and went to bed at eight o'clock.

11. Matt didn't even read under his covers with a (lhasftighl) _____.

Jack Sprat

Matt likes this funny poem about food. Read the poem aloud. Circle the rhyming words. Underline the words that have the **long e** sound in them.

Jack Sprat could eat no fat;

His wife could eat no lean.

And so between the two of them,

They licked the platter clean.

This is a list of some of the foods Denise and Matt like to eat. Put the list in alphabetical order.

pizza   _____

chili beans   _____

cheese   _____

beets   _____

peaches   _____

beef   _____

leeks   _____

celery   _____

green beans   _____

peas   _____

honey   _____

ice cream   _____

potatoes   _____

meat   _____

Your Food Poem

Use the poem about Jack Sprat and his wife as a pattern. Write your own poem about your favorite food. The poem should be four lines long, and each pair of lines should rhyme. Here is an example poem about one of Denise's favorite treats.

Chocolate is my favorite treat—

A luscious sweet I love to eat.

Chocolate kisses, minty creams—

I eat chocolate in my dreams.

Write your poem here:

_____

_____

_____

_____

_____

_____

_____

When you have finished your poem, read it to someone in your family.

Spelling Grade 3—RBP075X

ABC Food

Use food words you put in alphabetical order on page 26 to fill in the blanks below.

1. Matt thinks pepperoni _____ is delicious.

2. Denise likes peanut butter and _____ on bread as a snack.

3. Matt's family often has grilled _____ sandwiches with soup.

4. _____ _____ topped with fresh _____ is a summertime treat.

5. Matt and Denise like to eat _____ many ways: mashed, baked, and as hash browns.

6. On a cold winter day, Mother sometimes serves _____ _____.

7. Dad likes to grill ground _____ patties for supper.

8. Mother prefers that Denise snack on carrot and _____ sticks.

9. Fried chicken is Matt's favorite kind of _____.

10. _____ are a kind of onion Mother puts in potato soup.

11. Dad likes creamed _____ and potatoes for supper in the fall.

12. Mother makes a very tasty red soup using _____.

Little Miss Muffet

"Little Miss Muffet" is a poem Denise likes. She looked up the words *curds* and *whey* in the dictionary. Find those two words in the dictionary and write the definitions on the lines below.

Little Miss Muffet

Sat on a tuffet,

Eating her curds and whey;

Along came a spider,

Who sat down beside her,

And frightened Miss Muffet away.

curds:

_____

_____

_____

whey:

_____

_____

_____

Read the poem aloud. Circle the **short i** sounds. Underline the **long i** sounds.

Spelling Grade 3—RBP075X

Long and Short *i* Crossword

Use **long i** and **short i** words from the Word Bank to solve the crossword puzzle.

little	thin	miss	big
spider	still	give	children
frighten	right	line	different

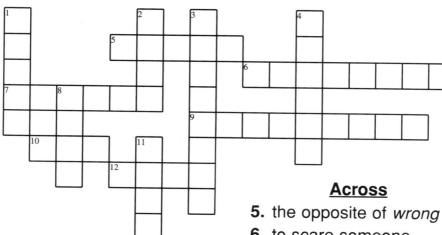

Across

5. the opposite of *wrong*
6. to scare someone
7. means the same as *small*
9. the opposite of *same*
10. the opposite of *little*
12. the opposite of *take*

Down

1. to be very quiet
2. When you go to lunch, you stand in a _____.
3. Boys and girls are _____.
4. the insect that scared Miss Muffet
8. the opposite of *fat*
11. When someone you love leaves, you _____ them.

30

Long o Poem

One night Denise's mother read this poem, which is also a riddle. See if you can guess what the poem is about. Then circle all of the **long o** sounds in the poem.

Little Nancy Etticoat,

With a white petticoat

And a red nose;

She has no feet or hands;

The longer she stands,

The shorter she grows.

Write the answer to the riddle here:

_____

Circle each word below that has the long o sound in it.

home	hot	to	show
long	old	going	town
own	note	not	froze
goal	young	comb	short

O Is for Opposites

Match each word in the first column with its opposite in the second column.

1. come   full

2. low   sad

3. young   go

4. little   short

5. light   hot

6. gentle   dirty

7. dry   big

8. tall   rough

9. clean   old

10. cold   dark

11. empty   high

12. funny   wet

Write the pair of opposites you read in the poem about Little Nancy Etticoat on the lines below.

_____   _____

-er and -est

The suffixes **-er** and **-est** are used to make comparisons.
Fill in the blanks in the sentences below using -er or -est.

1. John is short____ than Tom.

2. Bill is the short____ in his class.

3. Denise wants to know how much long____ the test will take.

4. Matt wants to know which is the long____ day of the year.

5. Jane is young____ than Michael.

6. Michael is the young____ in his family.

7. Denise is old____ than Matt.

8. Denise is the tall____ girl in her class.

9. Dan is the short____ boy in Denise's class.

10. Mom lit a candle because the storm made the day seem dark____.

11. The light from the flame made the room seem bright____.

12. The candle flame was growing small____.

13. The stove made the kitchen the warm____ room in the house.

14. Matt's campfire was the small____ in camp.

© RBP Books

Bryan O'Lin

Matt likes this funny poem about a man who made himself some clothes. Circle the rhyming words in the poem.

Bryan O'Lin had no breeches to wear,

So he bought him a sheepskin and made him a pair,

With the skinny side out and the woolly side in.

"Ah ha, that is warm!" said Bryan O'Lin.

Look up *breeches* and *sheepskin* in the dictionary, and write their meanings on the lines below.

breeches: _____

_____

sheepskin: _____

_____

Write the two words from the poem that rhyme with *air* on the lines below.

_____   _____

Now write a homophone for each of those words. Remember that homophones are words that sound alike but are spelled differently and have different meanings.

_____   _____

Homophone Crossword

Use the homophones in the Word Bank to solve the crossword puzzle.

bare	hair	pair	wear
pear	stair	stare	pare
bear	hare	ware	

Across

1. to peel a fruit or vegetable
2. another word for *rabbit*
3. without anything on it
5. something for sale
6. to look at something without blinking
7. a step that takes you up or down

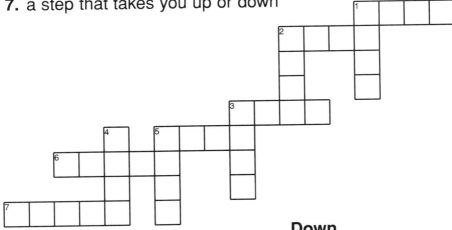

Down

1. a fruit that is white on the inside and yellow or green on the outside
2. This grows on your head.
3. one of the animals Goldilocks met
4. a set of two objects
5. what you do with clothes

Short *i* School Clothes

On the lines below, list the words from the poem about Bryan O'Lin that have the **short i** sound in them. Two short *i* words are used two times.

_____   _____   _____

_____   _____   _____

_____   _____   _____

light	linen	line	inch	silk	fine
thin	stitch	zip	spill	slip	style
crimson	pick	gift	big	size	

Use the Word Bank words that have the short *i* sound to fill in the blanks. Not all the words will be used.

1. Matt's pants were too short because he grew an _____ last year.

2. Matt got to _____ some new shirts for school.

3. Matt likes to wear shirts he can _____ over his head.

4. Matt tried not to _____ chocolate milk on his new shirt.

5. Mother had to _____ a seam in Denise's new dress.

6. The dress was made of _____.

7. It was a beautiful shade of _____.

8. Denise received a new pair of shoes as a birthday _____.

9. She had to take the shoes back and get some others because they were too _____.

10. Matt and Denise wear coats that _____ up.

11. Their shirts are made of _____.

12. Mother likes to wear clothes that make her look _____.

Old Mother Hubbard

Matt and Denise know a dog that makes them think of this silly poem. Circle the Word Bank words where they appear in the poem. Underline the rhyming words.

old	mother	went	her
said	get	she	the
him	came	there	made

Old Mother Hubbard

Went to her cupboard

To get her poor dog a bone.

But when she got there,

The cupboard was bare,

And so the poor dog had none.

She went to the barber's

To buy him a wig,

But when she came back

He was dancing a jig.

The dame made a curtsy.

The dog made a bow.

The dame said, "Your servant."

The dog said, "Bow-wow."

Spelling Grade 3—RBP075X

Mother Hubbard Word Search

Find the words you circled in the poem "Old Mother Hubbard" in the word search below.

old	mother	went	her
said	get	she	the
him	came	there	made

```
t q k j r r y l h i m e e r f j o
y h r c l n k h c h e r k o s l y
k x e r a z d m a d e e e t d d d
w m h a c m z e h s b h t k g t b
v i t e e e c t i t t u y r g v
e u o p i o o t y p n c s z r s e
h e m b w y a e a v e i d i a s f
t t k w r n k g d v w c o n o v j
```

www.summerbridgeactivities.com

Spelling Sentences

Write five sentences using some of the Word Bank words you found in the poem "Old Mother Hubbard."

1. _____

_____

2. _____

_____

3. _____

_____

4. _____

_____

5. _____

_____

Spelling Time Word Search

The grandfather clock in the hallway makes Denise think of this poem. Read the poem aloud. Circle the words that end in **-ck**.

Hickory, dickory, dock,

The mouse ran up the clock.

The clock struck one,

The mouse ran down,

Hickory, dickory, dock.

Find the Word Bank words describing time in the word search below.

yesterday	today	tomorrow	morning
afternoon	evening	daybreak	midnight
future	now	then	

```
f  d  w  w  x  w  i  b  r  p  t  j  u  g  g  n  r
m  i  d  n  i  g  h  t  w  n  a  y  j  c  n  g  c
e  a  f  t  e  r  n  o  o  n  b  l  q  e  i  n  d
l  r  x  c  f  k  a  e  r  b  y  a  d  h  n  i  h
o  y  u  u  y  w  t  o  d  a  y  i  q  b  e  n  u
w  o  n  t  n  e  h  t  z  o  g  c  u  i  v  r  y
d  d  u  h  u  p  w  o  r  r  o  m  o  t  e  o  v
c  g  l  q  a  f  y  e  s  t  e  r  d  a  y  m  l
```

www.summerbridgeactivities.com   ©RBP Books

-*ck* Word Puzzle

Solve the **-ck** word puzzle. The first one is done for you.

1. sack – s + st = _____ **stack**_____

2. stack – st + sh = _____

3. shack – sh + p = _____

4. pack – p + tr = _____

5. track – tr + l = _____

6. lack – ack + uck = _____

7. luck – l + tr = _____

8. truck – tr + m = _____

9. muck – uck + ock = _____

10. mock – m + cl = _____

11. clock – cl + kn = _____

12. knock – kn + r = _____

At the Cabin

Circle the correct word; then write it in the blank.

1. Behind the cabin is an old (shack/sack) _____ made of logs.

2. There is a (stack/struck) _____ of wood next to the cabin.

3. Mom told Denise to (pack/rock) _____ her bag for the camping trip.

4. Matt followed some deer (trucks/tracks) _____ in the woods.

5. Matt sat down on a (rack/rock) _____ to rest.

6. With a little (lack/luck) _____, he might see a deer.

7. Mom set the big (clock/cock) _____ on the wall to the correct time.

8. Denise saw a (truck/track) _____ pull into the driveway.

9. Soon there was a (knack/knock) _____ on the door.

10. Matt hung a calendar above his desk with a (tock/tack) _____.

11. "These cookies (lack/lock) _____ salt," said Mother.

12. Denise still likes her mother to (tuck/tack) _____ her in at night.

Long o, Long *i*, and Short *i*

Circle the words with the **long o** sound. Then under-line all the words in the Word Bank where they appear in the poem.

old	woman	under	there
she	still	never	

There was an old woman who lived under the hill,

And if she's not gone, she lives there still.

Baked apples she sold, and cranberry pies,

And she's the old woman who never told lies.

Write the **short i** rhyming words from the poem below:

_____   _____

Write the **long i** rhyming words from the poem below:

_____   _____

     Spelling Grade 3—RBP075X

Short *i* Word Puzzle

Solve the word puzzle below full of **short i** words.
You may recognize some of the words from the poem
about the old woman who lived under the hill.

1. still – ll + tch =   **stitch**

2. ditch – tch + ll = _____

3. will – ll + tch = _____

4. pitch – tch + ll = _____

5. hill – ll + tch = _____

6. sill – s + sp = _____

7. gill – g + gr = _____

8. till – t + tr = _____

9. trill – t + th = _____

10. dill – d + dr = _____

11. bill – b + h = _____

12. fill – f + b = _____

Many of the words you need to solve this crossword puzzles are homophones. They sound the same, but they are spelled differently.

lie	toll	tall	Thai
soul	sold	die	told
sole	dye	lye	tie

Across

2. The girl from Thailand spoke _____.

3. the bottom of a shoe

5. a strong chemical, sometimes used in making soap

7. To cross the bridge, the driver must pay a fee called a _____.

8. the past tense of *tell*

10. to stop living

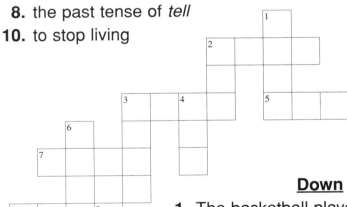

Down

1. The basketball player is very _____.

2. The race was a _____.

3. He _____ his car to his brother.

4. to say something that is not true

6. another word for *spirit*

9. to change the color of cloth or hair

A Man in the Wilderness

Circle the words in this poem that rhyme. Underline the **long e** words.

A man in the wilderness asked me,

"How many strawberries grow in the sea?"

I answered him as I thought good,

"As many as red herrings grow in the wood."

Write the two plural words from the poem on the lines:

_____   _____

Find the words *red herring* and *wilderness* in the dictionary. Write their definitions on the lines below.

red herring (it has two meanings):

1. _____

_____

2. _____

_____

wilderness:

_____

_____

A Passel of Plurals

Write the correct plural spelling for each of the singular words below. Look for words that are in the poem about the red herrings.

1. berry _____

2. house _____

3. story _____

4. school _____

5. strawberry _____

6. library _____

7. line _____

8. name _____

9. country _____

10. place _____

11. penny _____

12. world _____

13. herring _____

14. sea _____

Spelling Grade 3—RBP075X

It Rhymes with *Sea*

Circle the word in each group that rhymes with *sea*;
then write it on the line:

1. bed   tree   tread   _____

2. she   bell   shell   _____

3. say   bee   black   _____

4. friend   pen   free   _____

5. pencil   pea   pie   _____

6. flea   fast   fly   _____

7. cane   knee   kept   _____

8. wept   when   we   _____

9. me   men   maid   _____

10. two   three   ten   _____

11. hen   he   high   _____

12. fee   fry   find   _____

     ©RBP Books

There Was a Crooked Man

Circle the rhyming words in the poem. Underline the past tense verbs.

There was a crooked man

Who walked a crooked mile.

He found a crooked sixpence

Against a crooked stile;

He bought a crooked cat,

Which caught a crooked mouse,

And they all lived together

In a crooked little house.

Find *sixpence* and *stile* in the dictionary. Write the definitions on the lines below.

sixpence: _____

_____

stile: _____

_____

According to the dictionary, what country does the word *sixpence* come from?

_____

Crooked Man Word Puzzle

Discover the secret message at the bottom of the page by solving the word puzzles below. It uses words you will find in the poem about the crooked man.

1. purchased
      ___ ___ ___ ___ ___ ___
          1

2. _____ lived together.
      ___ ___ ___ ___
             2

3. The opposite of *ran*.
      ___ ___ ___ ___ ___ ___
          3

4. not straight
      ___ ___ ___ ___ ___ ___ ___
          4

5. a step over a fence
      ___ ___ ___ ___ ___
               5

6. a small gray rodent
      ___ ___ ___ ___ ___
      6

7. sounds like witch
      ___ ___ ___ ___ ___
      7

8. a place to live
      ___ ___ ___ ___ ___
             8

9. the opposite of lost
      ___ ___ ___ ___ ___
          9

Secret Message: ___ ___ ___ ___ ___ ___ ___ ___ ___ ___ ___.
             2 1 9 3 4 5 3 7 5 8 1 6 5

Money Crossword

Solve the crossword puzzle using "money" words you know.

buy	price	credit	nickel
penny	dime	quarter	dollar
bill	change	work	coin

Down

1. the cost of something
2. Ten cents makes one _____.
3. money you receive back when you buy something
4. a coin worth five cents
5. a piece of money made of paper
7. what you must do to earn money
8. another word for *purchase*

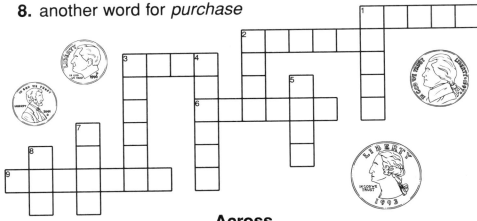

Across

1. another word for *cent*
2. Four quarters make one _____.
3. a piece of money made of metal
6. a way to pay without using cash
9. Twenty-five cents makes one _____.

51

Animal, Animals

If the animal name is singular, write the plural on the line. If the name is plural, write the singular form.

1. mice _____

2. rat _____

3. cats _____

4. fleas _____

5. dog _____

6. deer _____

7. horses _____

8. bunny _____

9. ponies _____

10. puppy _____

11. calves _____

12. bird _____

13. ducks _____

14. goat _____

15. sharks _____

Robbers!

Circle all the pronouns in this poem.

There was a man, and he had naught,

And robbers came to rob him;

He crept up to the chimney top,

And then they thought they had him.

But he got down on the other side,

And then they could not find him;

He ran fourteen miles in fifteen days,

And never looked behind him.

Find the word *naught* in the dictionary. Write the definition you find on the lines below.

naught:

_____

_____

Write a sentence using the word *naught*.

_____

_____

Spelling Grade 3—RBP075X

Crack the Code

Use the mystery code below to decipher the words from the poem encoded below.

Mystery Code												
♋	♌	♍	♎	♏	♐	♑	♒	♓	♈	♊	☹	💣
a	b	c	d	e	f	g	h	i	j	k	l	m
☠	♭	⚐	✈	☼	♦	❄	◆	❖	⊕	⊠	⊡	☾
n	o	p	q	r	s	t	u	v	w	x	y	z

1. ♒ ♏ _____

2. ♒ ♓ 💣 _____

3. ❄ ♒ ♏ ⊡ _____

4. ☼ ♭ ♌ ♌ ♏ ☼ ♦ _____

5. ♐ ♓ ♐ ❄ ♏ ♏ ☠ _____

6. ☹ ♭ ♭ ♊ ♏ ♎ _____

7. ☠ ♏ ❖ ♏ ☼ _____

8. ♌ ♏ ♒ ♓ ☠ ♎ _____

9. ♐ ♓ ☠ ♎ _____

10. ♒ ♋ ♎ _____

11. ☠ ♋ ◆ ♑ ♒ ❄ _____

12. ♍ ☼ ♏ ♭ ❄ _____

54

Measuring Up

Use the Word Bank to find the measuring words for land and travel in the word search below.

mile	meter	inch	yard
foot	centimeter	far	near
distance	across	long	short

```
l  d  f  i  z  k  h  a  w  m  n  o  t  o  o  f  h
o  w  r  m  c  e  n  t  i  m  e  t  e  r  n  h  t
n  q  v  a  a  c  r  o  s  s  k  h  f  n  f  a  r
g  h  k  t  y  q  s  e  c  n  a  t  s  i  d  v  h
n  l  r  f  r  r  e  t  e  m  r  n  n  w  i  o  n
e  z  a  a  u  i  r  d  e  c  m  s  u  n  m  i  k
r  c  e  f  e  k  t  r  o  h  s  l  c  e  l  i  m
t  n  m  k  f  e  y  j  i  x  t  h  x  v  w  x  d
```

Spelling Grade 3—RBP075X

Miles to Go

Write the plural on the line next to the word if the word is singular. If the word is plural, write the singular form.

1. miles _____

2. inch _____

3. feet _____

4. yard _____

5. meters _____

6. centimeter _____

7. point _____

8. maps _____

9. distance _____

10. locations _____

11. street _____

12. countries _____

Hey, Diddle, Diddle

Circle the rhyming words in this poem.

Hey, diddle, diddle,

The cat and the fiddle,

The cow jumped over the moon.

The little dog laughed

To see such sport,

And the dish ran away with the spoon.

Think of two more words that match each rhyme and write them on the lines below.

"iddle"   "oon"

_____   _____

_____   _____

The word *sport* has more than one meaning. The one we usually think of is "playing a game." Find another meaning for the word *sport* in the dictionary that fits the way the word is used in the poem. Write that meaning on the line below.

_____

Name That Tune

Use the Word Bank to help you unscramble the words in parentheses. Write the unscrambled word on the line.

bass	enjoys	lines	tap
read	snaps	harp	fiddle
sing	drum	flute	sound
spaces			

1. Denise is learning to play the (ddlief) _____.

2. Matt and Denise (ngis) _____ in the school chorus.

3. Mother plays the (utelf) _____.

4. She loves to listen to (rpha) _____ music.

5. You can always hear the (dnous) _____ of music in the house.

6. Mother taught Denise to (eard) _____ music.

7. She can say the names of all the (inesl) _____ and (acesps) _____ on the musical staff.

8. Father has a beautiful (bssa) _____ voice.

9. The family (jenoys) _____ singing together.

10. Matt sometimes (pasns) _____ his fingers to a catchy tune.

11. Matt wants a (umrd) _____ set for his birthday.

12. He likes to (apt) _____ out rhythms with his hands.

Old Mother Twitchett

Circle the rhyming words in the poem.
Underline the words with **short a** sounds.

Old Mother Twitchett had but one eye

And a long tail, which she let fly;

And every time she went over a gap,

She left a bit of her tail in a trap.

Write the answer to the riddle here:

_____

Look these words up in the dictionary and write the definitions that fit the way the word is used in the poem on the lines below. Then write a sentence using each word.

1. twitch _____

2. gap _____

_____

_____

_____

From A to Z

Put these words from the riddle in alphabetical order.

1. eye   _____

2. fly   _____

3. trap   _____

4. time   _____

5. mother   _____

6. left   _____

7. tail   _____

8. gap   _____

9. bit   _____

10. one   _____

11. went   _____

12. over   _____

Short *a* Picture Match

Write the correctly spelled **short a** word next to the picture it matches.

1.

_____

2.

_____

3.

_____

4.

_____

5.

_____

6.

_____

7.

_____

8.

_____

9.

_____

10.

_____

11.

_____

12.
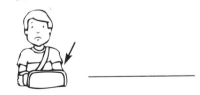
_____

13.

_____

14.

_____

Short *a* Word Puzzle

Solve the word puzzles below to create words containing the **short a** sound.

1. trap – tr + t = _____

2. bag – b + s = _____

3. sap – s + sn = _____

4. hand – h + l = _____

5. cast – c + l = _____

6. snap – sn + m = _____

7. bag – b + fl = _____

8. land – l + st = _____

9. van – v + m = _____

10. grass – g + b = _____

11. grass – gr + gl = _____

12. last – l + f = _____

13. stand – st + s = _____

14. plant – pl + p = _____

15. last – l + bl = _____

Tweedledum and Tweedledee

Circle the rhyming words in the poem. Underline the words with long vowel sounds in them.

Tweedledum and Tweedledee

Agreed to fight a battle,

For Tweedledum said Tweedledee

Had spoiled his nice new rattle.

Just then flew by a monstrous crow,

As black as a tar-barrel,

Which frightened both the heroes so,

They quite forgot their quarrel.

Make 15 words from the letters in "Tweedledum and Tweedledee." Be sure to check your spelling.

1. _____

2. _____

3. _____

4. _____

5. _____

6. _____

7. _____

8. _____

9. _____

10. _____

11. _____

12. _____

13. _____

14. _____

15. _____

Solve the **-ow** word puzzles below.

1. crow – cr + gl = _____

2. glow – g + f = _____

3. row + g = _____

4. low – l + kn = _____

5. row – r + t = _____

6. flow – fl + m = _____

7. tow – t + sh = _____

8. blow – bl + sn = _____

9. blow – b + s = _____

10. glow – g + be = _____

Use five of the words you just made solving the word puzzles in two or three sentences below.

_____

_____

_____

_____

_____

_____

Word Walk

Take a walk around your neighborhood with a friend or family member. Write a list of ten compound words that name objects, words on signs, or people you see.

Example: sidewalk

1. _____
2. _____
3. _____
4. _____
5. _____

6. _____
7. _____
8. _____
9. _____
10. _____

Long Vowel Favorites

Make a list of ten of your favorite foods that contain the long vowel sounds ā, ē, ī, or ō. Use the words to create your own word search. Give it to a friend to solve.

1. _____

2. _____

3. _____

4. _____

5. _____

6. _____

7. _____

8. _____

9. _____

10. _____

Word Search Review

Find each of the words in the Word Bank in the word search below. They are all words that appeared in poems and riddles earlier in this book.

pumpkin	curds	upstairs	candle
sheepskin	knave	whey	nightgown
breeches	time	strawberries	wilderness
sixpence	naught	robber	sport
gap	bit		

```
t  r  o  p  s  e  n  w  o  g  t  h  g  i  n
q  j  s  s  e  h  c  e  e  r  b  t  g  h  g
m  v  t  p  u  m  p  k  i  n  i  z  v  u  k
t  h  r  m  t  n  i  k  s  p  e  e  h  s  n
h  r  a  p  s  t  s  g  e  l  d  n  a  c  a
g  j  w  a  h  b  i  p  i  k  l  a  n  m  v
u  i  b  g  j  d  t  b  v  s  h  u  c  x  e
a  f  e  e  c  n  e  p  x  i  s  y  u  s  l
n  m  r  x  s  m  p  r  o  b  b  e  r  a  g
d  t  r  e  w  a  a  q  a  p  d  i  d  s  m
i  f  i  y  m  e  p  t  y  p  s  n  s  b  x
a  m  e  m  f  i  s  r  i  a  t  s  p  u  z
d  h  s  p  p  x  t  s  o  u  m  c  p  x  w
w  n  w  i  l  d  e  r  n  e  s  s  f  y  v
```

Over the Rainbow

Critical Thinking Skills

Spell at least 25 words from the letters in the phrase below. There are over 50 possible words. Use only the letters in the phrase. Use a letter no more times in one word than the number of times it occurs in the phrase. For example, there are five e's in the phrase. A word could at most have only five e's in it. If the letter is not in the phrase, you cannot use it in a word. For example, there are no l's in the phrase. Be sure to check your spelling.

"Somewhere over the rainbow"

1. _____   14. _____
2. _____   15. _____
3. _____   16. _____
4. _____   17. _____
5. _____   18. _____
6. _____   19. _____
7. _____   20. _____
8. _____   21. _____
9. _____   22. _____
10. _____   23. _____
11. _____   24. _____
12. _____   25. _____
13. _____

Spelling Bee Hangman

Need: Two teams of four to six players (or more)
Dictionary
Paper and pencils
Chalkboard, whiteboard, or large piece of paper (easel size)
Timer
Scorekeeper
Scribe

Each team member chooses a word from the dictionary and writes the word and its definition on a piece of paper.

Each team takes a turn trying to spell the word chosen by the other team.

Example:

Team 1 draws the hangman scaffold on the board so everyone can see it. Team 2 tries to guess the letters in the word within three minutes without being hanged. The team gets three points if they do. The scribe writes the letters Team 2 chooses on the board. After the three minutes are up, if Team 2 has guessed the word, they can earn two more points if they can tell what the word means in less than a minute.

Guessing is allowed.

Then Team 1 tries to guess a word Team 2 players choose.

Play until all the words each team has chosen have been used. The team with the most points at the end wins.

Create a Word

Follow the directions to create a new word.

1. An object used to hit a baseball   _____

2. Change the *a* to *u*.   _____

3. Add *t*.   _____

4. Add the suffix *er*.   _____

5. Add a word that means "to soar through the air."   _____

6. Change the *y* to *i* and add *es*.   _____

7. Draw a picture below of the the word you created.

Answer Pages

Page 1
1. Monday's
2. Tuesday's
3. Wednesday's
4. Thursday's
5. Friday's
6. Saturday's
7. Sabbath

Page 2
1. Sunday
2. Monday
3. Tuesday
4. Wednesday
5. Thursday
6. Friday
7. Saturday

Page 3
1. Sun.
2. Mon.
3. Tues.
4. Wed.
5. Thurs.
6. Fri.
7. Sat.

Answers will vary. Must be a riddle or poem about a day of the week that makes sense.

Page 4
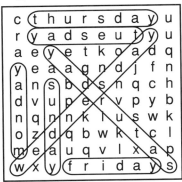

Page 5
30-days column: September, April, June, November

31-days column: January, March, May, July, August, October, December

28/29-days column: February

Page 6
ACROSS
3. May
6. September
8. January
9. August
10. July
11. December

DOWN
1. November
2. February
4. April
5. March
7. October
10. June

Page 7
January/Jan.
March/Mar.
May/May
July/July
September/Sept.
November/Nov.

February/Feb.
April/Apr.
June/June
August/Aug.
October/Oct.
December/Dec.

Page 8
Circled words: town, gown

Answer to riddle: daffodil

Any list of words that end in "own" and the long o sound.

Any springtime riddle using the "own" and long *o* sound words.

Page 9
Circled words: sat, went, down, came, ran, little, Catch, jumped, wall, him, got, what, said, away

Underlined words: tree, he, ran, can, wall, fall, say, away

Page 10
Circled words: eency, weency, spider, climbed, came, rain, spider, came, dried, rain, eency, weency, spider

Answer Pages

Page 11

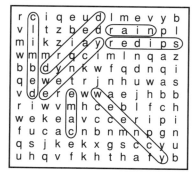

Page 12

1. bright
2. rain
3. try
4. clean
5. leaves
6. delight
7. beak
8. ray
9. rainbow
10. smile

Page 13

<u>tart</u>: a piece of baked pastry containing jam, fruit, etc.

Circled words: Hearts, made, tarts, day, Knave, stole, tarts, away, King, tarts, beat, sore, Brought, tarts, steal, more

Page 14

ACROSS	DOWN
3. moor	1. sore
4. soar	2. made
5. steel	5. steal
6. beet	6. beat
7. more	9. hart
8. maid	
9. heart	

Page 15

1. beach
2. seem
3. wear
4. sea
5. By
6. beet
7. sore
8. feet
9. know, wear
10. not

Page 16

1. ounce/oz.
2. teaspoon/tsp.
3. tablespoon/Tbsp.
4. cup/c.
5. pound/lb.
6. liter/l

tsp./teaspoon
oz./ounce
l/liter
Tbsp./tablespoon

Page 17

```
a h a l w x n o o p s a e t k z d
r w s c o o p x o f o e c i u j
y z l z c y g i y c o c u p c g x
b o c r s c m t a b l e s p o o n
q m e u h g n i v r e s x i n e t
k a n o a d n e l b e z t r i t s
m q y p k f n g d r b e c n u o n
n l g q e c i k l i m k y g m s r
```

Page 18

Circled words: light, bright, tonight, might, tonight

Answers will vary. Must be list of six words with the long *i* sound in them.

Answers will vary. Must be a four-line rhyming poem about stars or nighttime.

Page 19

1. To
2. r
3. sl
4. t
5. n
6. br
7. fl
8. l
9. s
10. l

Page 20

Circled words: Peter, Peter, eater, keep, He, he, very, Peter, Peter, eater, Peter, read, he, very

Underlined words: shell, there, kept, very, well, spell, then, very, well

Answer Pages

1. well
2. spell
3. keep
4. eater
5. wife
6. kept
7. another
8. shell
9. loved
10. Peter
11. read
12. pumpkin
13. had
14. very

Page 21
1. pumpkin
2. choose
3. crop
4. vines, dead
5. small
6. huge
7. fence
8. between
9. under
10. take, home

Page 22
Answers will vary. Must be six words that begin with the same consonant.

Answers will vary. Must be a tongue twister.

Page 23
1. pumpkin
2. very
3. read
4. loved
5. bell
6. kept
7. spell
8. well
9. wife
10. keep
11. shell

Page 24
Circled words: upstairs, downstairs, nightgown

1.	mid I night	mid	night
2.	day I light	day	light
3.	moon I light	moon	light
4.	night I gown	night	gown
5.	cart I wheel	cart	wheel
6.	play I ground	play	ground
7.	break I fast	break	fast
8.	day I break	day	break
9.	after I noon	after	noon
10.	stair I way	stair	way
11.	every I body	every	body
12.	any I thing	any	thing

13. class I room   class   room
14. side I walk   side   walk
15. chalk I board   chalk   board

Page 25
1. Everybody
2. cartwheel
3. midnight
4. daybreak
5. breakfast
6. classroom
7. chalkboard
8. playground
9. afternoon
10. nightgown
11. flashlight

Page 26
Circled words: sprat, fat; lean, clean

Underlined words: eat, eat, lean, between, clean

Alphabetical order:
beef
beets
celery
cheese
chili beans
green beans
honey
ice cream
leeks
meat
peaches
peas
pizza
potatoes

Page 27
Answers will vary. Must be a rhyming four-line poem about a favorite food.

Page 28
1. pizza
2. honey
3. cheese
4. Ice cream, peaches
5. potatoes
6. chili beans
7. beef
8. celery
9. meat
10. Leeks
11. peas
12. beets

     Spelling Grade 3—RBP075X

Answer Pages

Page 29

curds: the smooth, thickened part of sour milk sometimes used to make cheese

whey: the watery part of milk left when curds have formed and separated

Circled words: Little, Miss, Miss

Underlined words: spider, beside, frightened

Page 30

ACROSS	DOWN
5. right	1. still
6. frighten	2. line
7. little	3. children
9. different	4. spider
10. big	8. thin
12. give	11. miss

Page 31

Circled words: Etticoat, petticoat, nose, no, grows

Answer to riddle: a candle

Circled words: home, show, old, going, own, note, froze, goal, comb

Page 32

1. come/go	2. low/high
3. young/old	4. little/big
5. light/dark	6. gentle/rough
7. dry/wet	8. tall/short
9. clean/dirty	10. cold/hot
11. empty/full	12. funny/sad

Pair of opposites in poem: longer, shorter

Page 33

1. er	2. est
3. er	4. est
5. er	6. est
7. er	8. est
9. est	10. er

11. er	12. er
13. est	14. est

Page 34

Circled words: wear, pair, in, O'Lin

breeches: pants fitted below the knee

sheepskin: the skin of a sheep used with the wool still on and used as a rug or in a coat, slippers, gloves, etc.

Words rhyming with "air": wear, pair

Homophones: ware, pear/pare

Page 35

ACROSS	DOWN
1. pare	1. pear
2. hare	2. hair
3. bare	3. bear
5. ware	4. pair
6. stare	5. wear
7. stair	

Page 36

Short *i* words in Bryan O'Lin: O'Lin, him, sheepskin, him, With, skinny, in, is, O'Lin

1. inch	2. pick
3. slip	4. spill
5. stitch	6. silk/linen
7. crimson	8. gift
9. big	10. zip
11. linen/silk	12. thin

Page 37

Circled words: old, mother, went, her, get, she, there, the, him, came, made, said

Underlined words:

Hubbard	cupboard
bone	none
there	bare
wig	jig
bow	Bow-wow

www.summerbridgeactivities.com

Answer Pages

Page 38

Page 39
Answers will vary.

Page 40
Circled words: dock, clock, clock, struck, dock

Page 41
1. stack	2. shack
3. pack	4. track
5. lack	6. luck
7. truck	8. muck
9. mock	10. clock
11. knock	12. rock

Page 42
1. shack	2. stack
3. pack	4. tracks
5. rock	6. luck
7. clock	8. truck
9. knock	10. tack
11. lack	12. tuck

Page 43
Circled words: old, sold, old, told

Underlined words: old, woman, under, she, there, still, never

Short *i* rhyming words: hill, still
Long *i* rhyming words: pies, lies

Page 44
1. stitch	2. dill
3. witch	4. pill
5. hitch	6. spill
7. grill	8. trill
9. thrill	10. drill
11. hill	12. bill

Page 45
ACROSS	DOWN
2. Thai	1. tall
3. sole	2. tie
5. lye	3. sold
7. toll	4. lie
8. told	6. soul
10. die	9. dye

Page 46
Circled words: me, sea, good, wood

Underlined words: me, sea

Plural words: strawberries, herrings

Definitions:
red herring: 1. a dried, salted, smoked herring. 2. a subject used to divert attention

wilderness: an uninhabited, uncultivated area

Page 47
1. berry	berries
2. house	houses
3. story	stories
4. school	schools
5. strawberry	strawberries
6. library	libraries
7. line	lines
8. name	names
9. country	countries
10. place	places
11. penny	pennies
12. world	worlds
13. herring	herrings
14. sea	seas

75

Answer Pages

Page 48
1. tree
2. she
3. bee
4. free
5. pea
6. flea
7. knee
8. we
9. me
10. three
11. he
12. fee

Page 49
Circled words: mile, stile, mouse, house

Underlined words: was, walked, found, bought, caught, lived

sixpence: equal to six English pennies.

stile: a set of steps used by people to climb over a fence.

The word comes from Great Britain.

Page 50
1. bought
2. They
3. walked
4. crooked
5. stile
6. mouse
7. which
8. house
9. found

Secret Message: You are awesome.

Page 51
DOWN
1. price
2. dime
3. change
4. nickel
5. bill
7. work
8. buy

ACROSS
1. penny
2. dollar
3. coin
6. credit
9. quarter

Page 52
1. mice — mouse
2. rat — rats
3. cats — cat
4. fleas — flea
5. dog — dogs
6. deer — deer
7. horses — horse
8. bunny — bunnies
9. ponies — pony
10. puppy — puppies
11. calves — calf
12. bird — birds
13. ducks — duck
14. goat — goats
15. sharks — shark

Page 53
Circled words: he, him, He, they, they, him, he, they, him, He, him

naught: nothing, nothingness, zero

Sentences will vary. Example: He had naught but the clothes he wore.

Page 54
1. he
2. him
3. they
4. robbers
5. fifteen
6. looked
7. never
8. behind
9. find
10. had
11. naught
12. crept

Page 55

Page 56
1. miles — mile
2. inch — inches
3. feet — foot
4. yard — yards
5. meters — meter
6. centimeter — centimeters
7. point — points
8. maps — map
9. distance — distances

76

www.summerbridgeactivities.com   © RBP Books

Answer Pages

10. locations   location
11. street   streets
12. countries   country

Page 57
Circled words: diddle, fiddle, moon, spoon

Two words that rhyme with *diddle*; (Examples: fiddle, riddle, middle).
Two words that rhyme with *moon* or *spoon* (Examples: soon, tune, boon).

sport: to frolic or play

Page 58
1. fiddle   **2.** sing
3. flute   **4.** harp
5. sound   **6.** read
7. lines, spaces   **8.** bass
9. enjoys   **10.** snaps
11. drum   **12.** tap

Page 59
Circled words: eye, fly, gap, trap

Underlined words: had, And, gap, trap

Answer to riddle: a needle

twitch: to make a light, jerking pull

gap: an opening

Page 60
1. bit   **2.** eye
3. fly   **4.** gap
5. left   **6.** mother
7. one   **8.** over
9. tail   **10.** time
11. trap   **12.** went

Page 61
1. map   **2.** trap
3. lap   **4.** snap
5. man   **6.** fan
7. cap or hat   **8.** plant
9. flag   **10.** bag
11. van   **12.** cast
13. grass   **14.** hand

Page 62
1. tap   **2.** sag
3. snap   **4.** land
5. last   **6.** map
7. flag   **8.** stand
9. man   **10.** brass
11. glass   **12.** fast
13. sand   **14.** pant
15. blast

Page 63
Circled words: battle, rattle, crow, so (possibly barrel, quarrel)

Underlined words: Tweedledum, Tweedledee, Agreed, fight, Tweedledum, Tweedledee, nice, by, crow, frightened, both, heroes, so, quite

Possible words include:

weed	deed	led	mud
wed	weld	melt	duel
dew	let	ewe	wet
dwell	tweet	dental	mutt
tell	dell	mad	dame
mall	lame	needle	dealt
death	deal	lead	need
wall	neat	teen	wall
ant	tan	law	wade

Page 64
1. glow   **2.** flow
3. grow   **4.** know
5. tow   **6.** mow
7. show   **8.** snow
9. slow   **10.** below

Sentences will vary.

Page 65
Answers will vary.
Possible answers might include:

playground	treetop
streetlight	housewife
mailman	stairway
rainbow	sunlight
policeman	baseball

Answer Pages

Page 66

Answers will vary.
Possible foods include:

pie	cake	doughnut
peas	peaches	cheese
potatoes	lima beans	beans
bacon	ice cream	
maple syrup		

Page 67

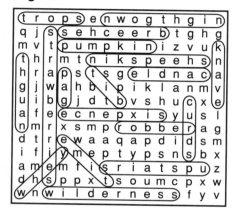

Page 68

Answers will vary.
Possible words include:

mare	some	here	bow
now	ban	ran	home
eat	there	ware	rare
share	roam	wear	bone
throne	went	vent	more
hare	steer	ear	swear
stone	rain	row	meat
wheat	beat	sweet	train
brain	vain	hen	bear
rent	tear	sore	bore
he	tree	rat	moan

Page 70

1. bat 2. but
3. butt 4. butter
5. butterfly 6. butterflies

The word is *butterflies.*